Other Works by
MATT MINOR

Magna Texannia

A Collection of Poems

MATT MINOR

Magna Texannia
Copyright © 2022 Matt Minor

dead tree

ISBN 978-1-7352249-7-8

Library of Congress Control Number: 2022903027

First Edition

10 9 8 7 6 5 4 3 2

Printed in the United States of America

Contents

INTRODUCTION

THERE REALLY IS NO SUCH THING as Modern Poetry. Poetry is an archaic practice. Whether it is measured verse or free verse, it is not of the industrial or technological age. Even in its most urbane form, there is something starkly primitive about it. And in its Augustan form, that verse which was strictly measured and balanced, it too preceded the industrial age. Put simply, poetry comes from a place that most moderns do not understand. This is because the place that poetry derives from is a place that eludes the mediocre creed of the civilized: Pragmatism and consumerism. Yet poetry is perhaps the most civilized of the arts, by the plain fact that it is wrought from language. It is not visual, nor is it necessarily audible (though it can be read aloud), but instead, written words. And language requires abstract thought.

Poetry, after cave painting, is the earliest of humankind's expressions. Initially poetry was oral, passed down from generation to generation as spoken word. This oral tradition, which exists in all cultures, usually recanted the daring and courageous acts of past warfare. Warfare was essential to ensure the survival of a respective tribe, as warfare for survival was an ugly fact of life. This oral tradition also recanted the actions of the natural world, in an attempt to explain the inexplicable. Respect for the natural world was essential, perhaps more than warfare, for the very existence of the tribe.

As the ages unfolded the art and craft of poetry developed into a sort of majesty. Poets evolved into the wizards, witches,

9

shaman, and witch doctors of legend. They provided council to chieftains, explained the inexplicable, authored creed, and treated the ill. In short: poets were the ancient equals to cabinet advisors, scientists, medical doctors, and lawyers. It was a golden age for the poet.

But the world grew up. And with that maturity, the poet's position in society declined. But it did not kill the notion of being a poet. And the notion of being a poet is the essence of what drives one to write poetry, whether the writer understands this or not. It is a connection to the workings of nature and of man; of the natural world and the patterns of human nature. To be a poet is to be a space traveler, to see the vast panorama of time itself. It may be ridiculous to us moderns, but it is my belief that this notion constitutes the guts of all great poetry. In fact, according to some Celtic myths, the Goddess, essentially a singular form of the Greek Muses, made her nest from the entrails of poets.

This naturally sounds esoteric to our modern ears. So, let me posit this notion in another way. I can think of no poetry that was inspired by mechanization alone. And to go further down this rabbit hole, consumerism, the final stage of capitalism, is certainly not an inspiration for the craft of verse.

In Late Western culture, consumerism has conquered all. And all is disposable. Art and knowledge, and even religion it can be observed, have no currency. The inevitable conclusion of consumerism is cultural nihilism. By reducing literally everything to an economic unit, we have destroyed the concept that things outside of the commercial square have any value whatsoever. Like it or not, this is where we, as a culture, have arrived.

Do not mistake me, I am not describing some backdoor excuse for Marxism. Whatever the flaws of global, consumer capitalism, it is a far better path than collectivism. Collectivism purges the very idea of the individual. It crushes identity. And identity is essential to any art form, whether it be of the representative or the romantic (anti-hero). In either instance, both notions are tied to a specific passion. The former is of place, the latter in opposition to it.

It is a quandary, and cannot be adjudicated. And so I come full circle: Poetry is an arcane practice. Still, some continue to write it. It is what makes us human, and separates us from all other species. As our technological age leaps from the Post-Modern into a Post-Human era (the natural extension), poetry, and the arts in general—if they can survive—may very well be our last stand against what we are increasingly beginning to believe is inevitable: our own annihilation through our own immaculate devices. Poetry is a form of protest, however foolish.

Matt Minor

5/24/21

NOTES ON THE TEXT

THIS COLLECTION OF POEMS spans nearly three decades. Though the bulk of those featured are more recent poems or pieces written in the last decade or so, there are a few that date back to the nineties, when I began writing poetry in earnest. The poems represented in this volume comprise only a small fraction of my total output through that duration.

Arranging the order of this collection was something of a challenge. At first I thought I might break the poems down into sections based on subject matter. Or, I had the obvious road of arranging them in chronological order based on date of composition. I decided against both these routes, and rather tried for a more organic contrivance: A rollercoaster ride through decayed columns, rural nooks, requited and unrequited love, and much more. It is up to the respective reader to determine if I made the right choice.

Many of these poems have been previously published in various publications across the country, but many more have not. Choosing what poems to include in this collection was difficult. And I consciously included those poems I personally value (though not all that I value), and that I believe have little hope of ever being published in our present cultural climate.

Many of these poems were written using strict meter, even rhyme. But some are not.

The final poem of this collection is a verse chronicle of the 87th Texas Legislature, which concluded on Memorial Day, 2021.

It began in January of that year and lasted to the end of May. The poem, if it can be called that, is a diary of my thoughts and temperament through those five taxing months. Anyone coming to the poem looking for great insight into the political process will be disappointed, as much of it details my sojourns away from the capitol, as well as those far from the city of Austin. Of its merits, I cannot say. It was an experiment that I decided to include in this collection.

Editing of this collection was minimal, as I tried to stay true to each original composition. However, some poems have been slightly altered from their original form.

Each poem has a date of composition affixed.

ACKNOWLEDGEMENTS

Visitation of the Forefather to the General's Tent on the Eve of Defeat, I Have Known Love Like the Lost Ancients, Garden of the Damned, A Southern Poet, Rural Ruins, The Committee Clerk, Dark Muse, Cutting Calves, Chimney Chapel, Before Their Time, The Return of the Anachronism, There is a Woman with an Ancient Soul, first appeared in *The Collection Too, featuring Matt Minor, Political Executive.* Published by the Houston Writers House (2016).

Leaves Drop Like Notes, first appeared in *The Lyric, the Nation's oldest publication dedicated to Traditional Poetry.* Vermont (Fall 2020).

Our Table, The Quiet Garden, To the Lawmakers, The Cave Painter, The Girl that I Hailed, first appeared in the novel, *The Singular Passion*, published 2020 (Dead Tree).

Flesh and Hubris, Meridian, The Futility and the Torment, first appeared in *The Collection.* 1st Place Poetry and Flash Fiction. Houston Writers House (2015).

She was a Girl and I was a Fool, Is Our Lovemaking a Confessional?, Her Cries Upon Climax, first appeared in the novel, *The Representative*, published 2014 (Dead Tree).

Southron Sage, first appeared in the *Simms Journal*. Winner of the Simms Poetry Competition. University of Georgia, Simms Society (2009).

On the Failure of US Presidents from the New South, first appeared in the *Deronda Review*. Madison, WI/Israel (2008).

Multiculturalism vs. The Melting Pot, first appeared in the *Fullosia Press* political and cultural journal. Rockaway Park, NY (2007).

In Search of Mother Earth, first appeared in *Smoke Signals*, Syracuse, NY (1992).

DEDICATIONS

(*In Memoriam*)

For Roger Paulding
...because you thought my poetry was 'wonderful'.
And more importantly, because you were
the indispensable curator of Texas letters.

To my brother Michael
Had we both just been born
in another time and another place...

To some distant, future generation,
who have acquired, after untold sufferings,
some notion of how to savor and celebrate life.

The Old Demons

The old demons never died, but rather slumbered
With one eye open, so as to watch our folly;
Feeding their dreams of reclamation and dominion.

Never startled awake, but rather lazy in their
Awakening, they yawn the yawn of the well-rested.
Their beastly sinews still taut with the memory of victory.

With a confidence never questioned, knuckles crack
And joints unstiffen. They need not map nor ugly news.
Because they, through the chasm of time, have never known
Defeat.

MHM

12/31/21

Magna Texannia (an oratorical)

I.

The spine of climbing civilization
Coils a sharp, double-edged, backward blade—
(The ever-present primacy of the cave)—
That pierces straight through coiling time.
Its pointed stone tip ever sharpening;
Growing with our hominoid tissue.

And often, very often…tissue bleeds.
Patching the plasma, intrepid you gloat…

II.

You've always been quite a rueful braggart,
It is both your charm and rank repellant.
But the businessmen, less the bricklayers,
Have always viewed your flexed bicep on the
Atlas as a tolerable point on
The greater, bloody, subjugated globe.

You were different really, kind of like France—
(An insult in the annals of insults?)—
Not to disregard your own invention,
You were and are a 'hive of industry.'
To ease your insult one can say you lack
The magic of the heirs of ancient Gaul.

But enough of the insults, you are great.
By your own grand contrivance, you are.
Your tragic flaw your lack of dimension.
Though you are good at hacking into earth,
It took west coast, post-modern hackers to
Hack your future, to undermine all.

III.

There are other endeavors to be sure:
Medicine; engineering; insurance.
You're good at pragmatism, very good.
But why not the impractical: the arts?
Not that you are bereft of genius.
(Why import your exports, after the fact?)

With your great aptitude for enterprise
Why could you not conjure competition;
Compete with the East for the portly ear?
Instead you groveled for their approval.
Your institutions of higher learning
Playing the role of Sparta to their Athens.

IV.

I remember when I became conscious
That I was a Texan. It made me proud.
My guitar like a lyre, strung vast dreams.
Weaving like a flag an empire vast,
Clothing the greater globe with novelty.
I fit a cauldron from your cowboy hat.

V.

The spine of climbing civilization
Will sever sometimes, epoch to epoch.
Not from your design, or your lack of grand
Imagination, your Western elders
Jabbed deep that stone-age tip, at your innards young;
Robbing you of your place…with the Ages.

12/7/20

Outlaw Reason

Here, where squared reason rots an outlaw,
We search through the aftermath for remnants
For the structure we learned, far far too late,
That without, we cannot feed ourselves.

Fallen monuments do not heed the soup
Spoon or salad fork, though we've chiseled their
Noses. Still we savor the collected rain
Water from the eye sockets, drinking their tears.

Why does it not satiate? We wonder.
History, that we have desecrated,
Demands that our parched lips can only be
Mollified by the letting of endless blood.

The heart's curvature, guided by touch,
Swings like a pendulum between extremes:
Love or hate? Hate or love? Neither do we feel.
Instead we grope the obelisks, feeding.

6/18/20

Visitation from the Forefather to the General's Tent on the Eve of Defeat

(a Southern Gothic)

Is not war enough of a nightmare?
But to be rattled awake while in tent
By an accusatory Shade floating on sod...

Was it Washington or Jackson, or whom?
Too difficult to tell through tortured eyes;
Buckles or boots? Powdered wig or shock of mane?

And what consternation in the Shade's reproach
At you, the *true* father of ambiguity;
And the bigotry, your orphaned offspring.

Patriot or traitor? The terms rendered
Meaningless in the musky July heat.
Reborn: Excommunication, in the predawn.

And for what? Heroes are not eternal,
And their progeny unreliable.
What, what did your sacrifice impart?

If the North and East were endowed with
Privilege. And the West: immortal freedom;
What the South...a sentiment out of time?

Or sweet tea...stock car racing...football?

How were you to know that Gentlemen would die
Like a virus to be inoculated.
A world you had not the resource to see.

Oh the scolding…the sordid reproach…
Maps draped over stoic tables claimed witness
To History's hunger for irony…

But how could that venerable Shade have known
That your defeat was in fact his own:
That fairness and defeat are together sown.

05/16

Dragons Breath

Time is accelerating.
And the dragons at the ends of earth gobble the taper.
Gather what you can and quickly.
The fog is not fog but encroaching smoke.

Try not to ponder the years we wasted
As if the years would never pass.
The masonry of memories will torture.
And there is little room and we've much to pack.

Only the knowledge of ages, or what we can cobble,
Will fit. Fugitive thought that we must covet:
Our debt till the grave to pay our penance
To the brick and mortar of an age we aged away.

Red enflames the horizon.
I do not know the way out.
But I would rather die on a frozen hillside
Clutching creation,
Then remain here awaiting the dragons' breath.

2/13/19

Chester

I think we might have had a chance
If Chester hadn't gone the way he went.
Might have had a chance at a second chance
If Chester had died in a knowing way.
But he vanished the night you, in impetuosity,
Let him out into the country night…
Because the traffic from the city,
The frustration of the day's relentless insistence,
Had brought you to breaking.

You never forgave yourself for letting him out.
Just a tiny kitten, barely weaned when we found him,
My persistence usurped your resistance.
And so we snatched him from the slimy culvert.
It was my gift to you to fill the emptiness I knew
 Consumed you.
But when he went, that was it really.

Sometimes alone, in the dark cabin we once
Together called home…I think I hear a shrill.
And stepping out into the hooded wood,
I hope to find a skinny orange cat
Clutching not mouse nor mole, but something else…
Something struggling in the weeds,
He found prancing along his way…
 Something of ours.

 And snatching it up…
 Returns your love.

2019

Meridian
(From the Texas Capitol at Austin, 84th Legislature)

How his meridian seemed a nadir:
With bruises swelling beneath a tired eye;
Undertow like a hangover dragging
Behind his ankle: a fallen sail.

He could starkly see with a bird's eye view
His drifting bark from the kingdom of clouds.
With blistered lips and bleeding index bent
He cursed the map he felt compelled to trace.

Black night brought strange relief, a paradox:
Indifferent stars bubbling like lager blond.
Blind undulation masking an atlas
And the splitting light which yielded no land.

5/15

The Limits of Freedom

In the age of the Founders, even the elite knew the meaning
  Of hardship and deprivation:
Thin firewood, shortage of wax, dearth of light, gout and
  missing teeth.
The notion of Freedom itself was a novelty to be dreamt
  And coveted for fear of death.
And death was as the reaper, harvesting bones as the
  scythe swept grain.

How could they have dreamt that their dream would fill
  silos of gluttony,
  And their words unleash ignorance:
Masses of fattened brats spitting on their inherited spoils.
The notion of commerce scarcely saw beyond the rudiments
  Of life's climbing brick and mortar.
Luxury was the sum of Monticello or a tall ship yard.

Fat cells multiply and the ailing blood and heart poison
  the flesh
  And debase the quick waning mind.
As art and inspiration once had the muscle of immortals,
Today it is reduced to a fiscal unit with less worth than
  A roll of white toilet paper.
And like Liberty, is flushed away with the spoil: Disposable.

4/11/21

Leaves Drop Like Notes

Leaves drop like notes from the ivories' suite.
The wind rustles like the whirling of strings.
The thinning sun mourns like a trumpet lone.
The yearning shadows lean like an oboe.

And the heart…? It pounds like a kettle drum.

In summer the sun I curse; loathe the moon in winter;
Impugn the spring for the fallacy that was…
But in fall I recall that memory of her:
A song inside only; tears for applause.

10/30/18

Idyll on Houston Street Apt. #2

Through a shrub-skirted mud alley bordering
The barrio, having just visited—
Along with the cats—the communal dumpster,
Toward the railroad tracks I watch the train track
Its way westward into obscurity.

Four mute seasons I have passed in this place.
My words are scarcely innumerable.
My pale pages starved of inspiration.
Questions countless curl the mind—why is this?

Some blank nights I'm stirred from frugal plugged sleep,
In twilight trance I hear, not the herald
Of an engine, but a ram's twirled horn,
Wailing from a long ship—(oar and water one)—
Merging into a mystic fjord or firth.

9/10/20

I Rue the Day We Let the World In

I always thought that as the world unraveled,
And Time's necrotic fangs fed on the thread,
And the tongue forked savored the undead,
Together, as apart, we would travel.

But our journey diverged like the world around,
From our welcoming the serpent that winds
Through the marital room labyrinthine:
A circle, alas, not perfectly round.

Was our bond loosened by time or sin?
No: These, the symptoms, not the catalyst.
It wasn't something missing but something missed.
I rue the day we let the world in.

12/17

Our Table

Under awning odd but humble,
Just an amble from my office,
Stands the Old Railroad Café.

In those May days that were brighter,
When we began, before the spleen,
Having never been, you wished to.

Against a century old, orange
Wall high, adorned with Texana,
Together we made our table.

I always knew how to find it,
When we returned, the times we did:
Near the rusted climbing trellis.

It was always so natural
Sharing a meal, the two of us:
You, ordering plain; me picky.

Should you wish again to lunch there…
Rue the day, I know I will…
Should we find our table is taken.

6/10/18

Inked Wings
(Requiem for the Rebellious Mind)

When writers behind the Iron Curtain,
Having fed off their own blood to create
Not Truth from Beauty, but Truth from chains,
Knew well that soon the fanged state would circle,
Gave flight their tomes of spirit and attack;
A scroll in the mouth of a free born bird,
Launched in desperation at the heirs of
Magna Carta, or across the big water,
Birthed from the thighs of an Age of Reason...
Knowing that binding awaited their ink.

No more will the bird touch terra firma
Welcoming of the sufferings of
The scribbling oppressed. Hiding in
The womb of self-absorption, we cannot
Hear the flapping in the cage. Our culture
Has poisoned our commonality. A
Trillion tiny neuroses we seek to
Justify our gluttony as we look East.
The nourishing placenta has dried hard
And crusted. The true meal of man is man:
The voice, the serifed hand, the crooked fingers,
And all the lean sufferings of the world.

Are the true tragedies of the world
Wingless to us now...just grindings for pulp?

3/3/21

Extinction

The stench of death pervaded the hall.
The cracked foundation slithered with snakes.
Nothing was, as it seemed: Truth was extinct.

The mildewed columns bred putrefaction.
Illness oozed from the water well.
Nothing was, as it seemed: Soul was extinct.

The childless lawn was stunted in growth.
The garden staples bore sores of disease.
Nothing was, as it seemed: Heart was extinct.

The Rubicon breached, the hall in sight...
No Judas, no Brutus, no destiny...
Nothing was as it seemed: God was extinct.

6/5/11

Heart Surgery
(for Sandra)

It was an odd obstacle that hovered between us,
What I believed a sort of miasma
That weighted the very air we breathe.
A mist made up of one part your shyness
    and the other…my arrogance.
Kissing I deemed its cure and thus administered,
From my lips to yours like a surgeon arcane.

But I was wrong in my diagnosis.
Though a mist it was it was not what I thought,
Rather our mutual wound located not at the mouth,
But in a place that beats involuntary…
Beats despite itself…until it can beat
    no more.

And it was lying beside you that I abandoned
All thoughts of cure and ailment,
All notions of righting an unjust world;
But finding contentment in the darkness,
Our limbs wrapped in ways the sick or saved
    could never hope to know.

9/8/19

Wasted Time?

Was our love, our life together, just wasted time?
Twenty long years and no legacy to show?
Only some cats whose graves are weeded wild over,
Moles and armadillos having made a home there…
Is this what marks our time after all this time?

They were good cats, all of them: Each individual.
And you loved them with a mother's love.
But they are gone as you too have gone away.
Living a life apart from mine,
As they merge below
With the ground they made mischief above.
The ground you no longer wish to walk on.

No children to claim our name or features.
Not your eyes, God forbid my nose –
No bones to sprout towards the heavens,
No minds the shape of meteors waiting
To harness what fire we could impart…

Nothing…nothing but this life apart.

11/30/18

The Heresy of Originality

A raucous trial of energy without redemption:
A beast on the run from bigger beasts,
At the water's tranquil edge, cut down at last…
A Tantalus in life, a Tantalus in death.

Out of the cauldron, or rather a cowboy hat,
Spawned an impossibility of opposites.
A dialectic the world will not reconcile.
Accident of birth; Mistake of Place and Time.

For the mind is not its own place
    —Milton you were wrong!
Age devours age as predators on the steppe.
And dreams are nightmares when day
    Is cloaked in darkness,
And anti-reality governs the willing herd.

What did you hope to accomplish by your design?
What gave faith to believe the blind could ever see?
Thus your heresy of originality…?
You should have known the teeth of exile moistened.

And so the gavel falls, like the jaws of injustice.
Your sustenance out of reach everlasting.
The liquid pumping legs outpaced by the pack:
A raucous trial of energy without redemption.

5/7/19

Flesh and Hubris
(From the Texas Capitol at Austin, 84th Legislature)

The firm boot steps on the marble tile
Project an alluring, measured cadence.
But their broadening echo is finite.

Chatter crescendos, ascending the dome,
Then fluttering like doves trapped in a house,
Exhausts itself, desperate for the light.

But if light is possible here at all,
It is by anecdotal accident.
For even the rat can negotiate
His fleshy nibbles through scarcity.

And flesh here is as scarce here as the light;
One's own face staring back from the language:
Bloodless words: panes pandering illusion.

5/15

The Wild Night the Astros Won the Series

The wild night the Astros won the Series
We met at Gringo's in fair Rosenberg.
I was hopeful and you were stark weary,
For you knew it would be a frozen dirge.

The pendant of an owl swung from your neck,
Like a wise portent; words yet uttered.
Syllables loosed on a life you would wreak.
Spoken with clarity, never muttered.

The cheer without belied the guts within.
The owl was *my* gift. Would it refuse to rave?
But upon your breast it heaved with the win.
Warm as the autumn, but cold as a grave.

12/17

The Muted Foggy Morn

The muted foggy morn
Cracks open its contents,
Like a thick runny egg
Over fence and field.

A tired troubled hand
Draws back the long curtain
Like hair from a fresh face;
Revealing ancient eyes.

Seething with a solace,
A solitude at ease,
Like a water painting,
Sky washes into land.

Smells from the small kitchen
Pervade the cottage home,
Like a timelessness told.
A kind wife cooks breakfast.

10/10

We Will Find It Now Alone
(for Sandra)

Deprived ascension by our date of birth,
Locked in a time dedicated to death,
We live in the long shadow of giants.

Meticulous the right angles of laid
Brick, zigzagging up to eternity...
Or so we thought. Who would have ever thought

That the green moss would eat the monoliths;
That ignorance could conquer intellect;
That love could be judged by the politico?

In my youth when I dreamed a young man's dreams,
I dreamed of a gold and silver castle
Where love and intellect together prospered...

We will find it now alone.

8/11/20

I Have Known Love Like the Lost Ancients

I have known love like the lost ancients.
A thing scorned by the money-eyed maniac.
A thing ignored by the print sentient,
But a thing far beyond all feigned attack.

Something against the world—a defiance;
That which made stronger by alienation.
Before bills, taxes and numbing Science;
That which exists as a separate nation.

But Love's bold secession is always crushed,
As Eden was foiled by pure innocence.
That rendered sallow which was once so flush:
An organism doomed to decadence.

I have known love like the lost ancients:
Lost to Life's hammer, ensconced in a fence.

2007

Garden of the Damned

There was nothing here for him
    But disappointment and dread.
The Edenic sun had set and the cold damp grass
    Swelled at his handsomely fashioned feet.
Still, the once white statues, now stained like lead,
 Along with the gray garden,
    Demanded he take a seat.

The mildewed bench would
    Blacken his pressed pants,
So he wiped the slime as if seeking for a name.
    A name on a long neglected tomb.
The scene had changed little from what scant
He remembered; its melancholy intact.
    His skin shivered through its bloom.

A bending branch seemed to
    Lean towards his lone figure
As if to accusingly ask, "Can you not save me?"
    The stiff people muttered their promise:
His flaming mind sent demons astir
Into the quickly advancing night.
    A night stained and ominous.

The stone bench, from beneath him
    In a voice familiar called,
"Woe to those damned on earth; their
    Damnation their heart's only salvation."

A dead raccoon, by mad coyotes mauled,
His tongue having harnessed the dank wind,
   "This garden is privation."

Like armor, his attire strove,
   To shield his flesh from the night.
Reminding the man of obligations
   To an impatient, abstract dime.
Out into the piss-hued phony light,
The gate behind still fluttering open,
   Upon his trousers he wiped the slime.

2008

The Great Fat Bird

I have seen the great fat bird only once:
Over the oval lake behind the house,
A silhouette in the murky moonlight,
Suspended like a dreadful frayed zeppelin.
I have heard, on anxious evenings alone,
Unable to sleep…consumed with fears,
The rustle and thump of its clumsy landing
In the blue woods that ensconce the waters.
Or, I have been jarred from troubled sleep
By a screech, as jagged as shattered glass,
Carving its ominous timbre on the
Spongy air saturated with darkness.
Wisdom, the owl brings, wrapt in elder
    wings…
All of it startling and born of night.

2007

A Southern Poet
(for Donald Davidson)

How he envied those that could break away,
Leave her cold, without longing or regret.
But the fat of sentiment too much weighed;
His brain grooved and the ink vivid long set.

What was it that kept him looking Southeast?
Was Weaver* right about the bounds of place?
Yet even Weaver and Ransom** could lease
Life apart, to quietly contemplate.

But for him the Grey dead had never sunk;
Art, a banner, not to push but to plant.
More the soldier than the stone musing monk:
Section of Earth rather than thoughtful cant.

The pious, right knew, in truth, however,
For the past to the past remained tethered.

* Dr. Richard M. Weaver *(The Southern Tradition at Bay),*
Student of JCRansom; later a professor at the University
of Chicago.
** Dr. John Crowe Ransom, Founder of both the Fugitive
Poets and the Southern Agrarian school of philosophy.
Though an undergraduate, and later teacher at Vanderbilt,
he was a Rhodes Scholar at Oxford and at last taught at
Kenyon College in Ohio.

2007

Rural Ruins

A solitary chimney amid mesquite;
Its hearth extinguished, its settlement lost.
Rising from thistle, the silent arm of
An old oil well, its scent no longer
Lingering stout in the fresh blue breeze.
Crenellated silos, orange corroded cars,
A tin barn thatched with a hundred autumns.
Mice, rats, opossums and snakes comfortably
    housed.
All the works of past ingenuity,
Their arrogance humbled by elements.
All the activity of past scheming,
Their plans forgotten like their yearning
    selves.

As rotting haystacks in the summer heat
All endeavors, foul or fair, Earth shall eat.

11/08

The Committee Clerk
(From the Texas Capitol in Austin, 83rd Legislature)

As confounding words and terms flew about—
Constructed from our lives impossible—
Flanked on both sides by a troop of old men,
Sat a creature out of her element.

And draped behind her like Liberty's own robe,
With the state seal perched like a bronze sun;
The Lone Star flag hung, languidly alone.
Her blue eyes intent, her small ears open.

All of his life he had projected art.
Bestowed beauty within, based from without.
Her poise should have passed but dallied about,
Her fingers would type, the eyes still intent.

Through circumstance, associates they were,
Seldom a private word between the two.
He would study her from the audience,
Their meeting eyes dashing quickly away.

Still, it wasn't her poise as much as her stain:
The breast's small, the blemished complexion:
The balance of imperfection and grace.
The blue eyes still intent, but not towards him.

3/13

A Civil Servant

Did politics smudge his humanity?
'Love' a word smeared unclear
    by a thumb print?
The same stamp that defined his dead position?
A stance that was peculiar to him alone?

The whispering green had cooled to silence,
And long ago red lips unrequited,
By the woman long beside him, had been hushed:
The risky irony of safe acceptance.

True, the naked hoard, chewing up
    wire and cloud,
Had numbed the rallying fist and flag.
But a subtle fire from the oppressed
Might thaw a fingertip charitable.

If only the grip were not too tight:
This host teetering between fire and ice.
A weak balance enflamed by tragedy...
Relieved by the coldness of five o'clock.

11/16

Mutinous Lover

In wakeful exhaustion I unsheathe from bed
Each morning, craving a cup of coffee.
And there in silence, that old dawning dread
Of a stifled future…far from lofty.

The mind numbed…
Thoughts charred…
The world has changed and I have not changed with it.

And I have had my legs cut from under me
So many times, that I question, just maybe,
I should surrender myself to crawling?

I have tried to fasten a forward poem
Celebrating our false ascendency.
The language wove to rot, words rebelled…
And what I wrought was a blade thrusting inward.

I won't act as laureate for winter's faux leaf.
I have found my edge playing the mutinous lover.
Aiming at the heart and my lone, sole belief:
That one can find love lasting…in another.

11/6/19

The Girl that I Hailed

I who understand the burning contempt cold,
Of labor without reward:
A tune caught as light ignites a snaking stream,
That I could never ford.
Or a conjured verse from the cauldron buoyant,
Yet scalded every word.
A legislative ends, plain, fair and just,
A governor deemed absurd…

But most contemptuous, by far, of all these fails…
The Love unrequited, from the girl that I hailed.

8/15/18

Dark Muse

There is still that sudden sash of color,
But now the focusing eye struggles to define
What once could not be contained.
Like the child who desired age
That Dark Muse drove you from the woods,
Robbed you of the laurel you hungered to cherish.
Words should float like feathers to the page
Not be shot from the sky in a fit of rage:
Poets are not gunfighters.
True that first taste of blood is always inspiring
But gun smoke does not trace pictures
As passing clouds can.
So all that you are left with is desert,
A desert dry and dead.
And not the blood from the fresh body below
Nor the swollen cacti
Will wet your lips with redemption.

1997

Cutting Calves

Cattle egrets gave way to buzzards black,
Waiting on limb and wire for mealtime.
For a heifer in a dash defiant,
Jutting her front hoof into a grassy hole,
Had snapped the tired limb terribly in two.
The slow rancher both alarmed and aloof,
Feigning the customary, 'aw shux,'
Stood ill-suited for this fresh errant charge.
The poor cow, mad with fear, panic and pain,
Mooed into the stillness of twilight pink.
"Got a pistol I can borrow from ya?"
The rancher asked with a crack in his drawl.
Handing him my .38, stepping back,
Her clueless head swallowed the single shot.
Thick blood poured from the panting nostrils,
But still the heifer tan struggled to stand.

"I think you need to shoot her again!" I shout.
"Don't want-ta waste yer bullets." He replies.
Seizing the pungent gun, stepping forward,
I drain the cylinder into her temple.
With drunken, woozy eyes, the head collapses.
The poor shaking body sends shivers blue.
The rancher, fitting a chain around the neck,
Through the dell, drags her limp into the wood.
The calf-stuffed diesel cars rumble awake…
Pink falls to purple, then purple to pitch.

8/09

How the Room Quickly Vanquished the Gloom

How the room quickly vanquished the gloom
    With new morning light,
As it shot exaltingly through my bedroom,
    Capturing the East
Like a snapshot taken by accident.
    While morning music,
Turning on the turntable ancient,
    Prepared a dreamer
For another school day of daydreaming;
    Prepared a lover
For another day of grace and meaning.

I thought it would last forever, I thought.
    Believed happiness
Dwelt somewhere in the circle I had wrought.
    Forgetting my room
My upstairs room at the front of the house,
    Behind the pillars,
Was built in the shape of a square Faust.
    A deal in numbers.
A deal a dreamer could never sign.
    A deal in doubt.
A deal this lover smeared with red wine.

Intoxicated as I was with remedies,
    (Not understanding
That art and happiness are enemies)
    These pillars I fled.
Taking much for granted my old square room,

Thinking light a right,
I found many a quarter filled with gloom.
After the folks died
I kept the old place out of sentiment,
But the sun had moved.
So I sold it, and all the money spent.

10/10

Poem in August

You have a great talent for making
    a mess of your life.
Me, I've known great moments, but never
    good times?
And as a woman good times sought you out,
But mostly you chose the larder gross
    over fine rhymes.
Yet life is a fool's story told over
    and over again.
Idiots are not needed, we've only to
    enlist the bright.
And the season may claim we were the among the brightest…
As long as our earth is spoiled…
    Laved in a thing called light.

8/8/19

Colonists
(for Sandra)

I wish I'd met you earlier,
Before the onset of autumn,
Before the orbiting earth
accumulated rings,
Before the bones and flesh
Felt the effects of physics.

But here we are, once having been adrift,
Finally finding ourselves with one another.

We the displaced: Each heart having fled
Its once settled territory.
For the heart is but a colonist,
Capable of setting off and founding
Ever more colonies.

And Lady this, I dearly wish…
To be a sturdier settlement.

9/12/19

The Quiet Garden

The State Seal both fed and exiled him:
Feeding his need for the body politic,
Yet standing sentry to the quiet garden
Green on the periphery of his imagination.

He could see her, smell her, and hear…
Her soft breathing ensconced within
The cursive gate that teased like a torso.
But he could not touch her, nor taste her.

Often he thought, as he stared through
   The coiled bars,
That he would trade the former senses
   For the latter.

But were not the lips and skin he so desired,
Not within but without?
Was not the soft breath he heard merely an echo
Tempting him back into the fight?

5/28/18

Recent Rains

The recent rains have lifted the Burn Ban.
Piles smolder in the damp heavy air.
The velvet taste of trees in every swallow.
Wood smoke snakes its way
    through the living wood,
Perfuming the forest like a damned witch.

Green is the base color of enchantment,
Smoke the mellow trail of ancient allure.

Simple the vessels needed to return
The knowledge that lingers in the senses.

10/09

In the Spartan Rooms of a Stoic Heart

In the Spartan rooms of a Stoic heart,
That pleases the blood opulent beating;
Through valves, whose only table is draped with
A silent flag dangling indifferent as
The idea ancient it symbolizes,
There you will share a meal that satisfies.

No ideal, brought into action, will not
Disappoint, bewilder or disillusion.
No chain, canon, or bright mushroom cloud
Can redeem the excuse that lit the wick.
There is no salvation in a nation,
Only the enduring past that complains.

Yet this table, sketched to hyperbole,
Set only with sad plates and tarnished
Cutlery, has set atop it the sole
Morsel needed for living consumption.
What if the idea was not an idea
At all…but the dull comfort…of one's end.

11/18/20

Vultures'-Eye View (atop Calvary)

VULTURE THE FIRST (flying behind)
All is a vast grand emptiness.
No Avenue that is not fraudulent;
No stair whose sharp steps are not set with skulls;
No hill that is not creased with streams of blood—
As is this one, that we orbit above.

VULTURE THE SECOND (flying ahead)
What is that? Do you hear what I'm hearing?

VULTURE THE FIRST
You mean the crass groans of the crucified?

VULTURE THE SECOND
No, I hear that too! I mean the music!

VULTURE THE FIRST
Suffering is my music, carrion my scale!
If that is what you mean, I do—yes!

VULTURE THE SECOND
No! I hear a swirling, a promenade
Not of the sentry but of something far
Off and from the future. It must be from
A time not yet known. It makes the hard heart
Beat like our flickering wings—coming from
The West! Oh it is genius and freedom!

VULTURE THE FIRST

Freedom? Freedom is a fraud...decadent
And never given out equitably.
Whatever you hear...wait...I hear it too!
It is impressive. It makes me want to
Continue circling and savor like death.

VULTURE THE SECOND

But it isn't the sound of death, it is
The sound of humans reaching their
Potential. Now the music is painting
Pictures! I see buildings of scaling glass!

VULTURE THE FIRST

I see nothing. And I will disregard
These visions of yours. Please act according
To your nature—like the humans. They are
Incapable of grandiosity.
And when they soar, it is for a brief time.
I'm zooming in now. I sense the reek of
The waiting grave. Say, which one of the three?

VULTURE THE SECOND

I can't hear you through the swooping song!
I cannot see for the blinding beauty!
As if through a portal I see the sun
Shining in the shape of a crucifix!
The one in the middle, he is not of flesh!

VULTURE THE FIRST

That's the one I'm angling for, the one in
The middle—a bit gangly, but the weak
One's perish with little life resistance.

VULTURE THE SECOND

Be careful, my love, there is something strange
About that one. Instinct speaks he is the One!

VULTURE THE FIRST

What, what is this? Something charges me back.
He is like a battlement self-contained.
I'm aborting him for the rogue on left.

VULTURE THE SECOND

I'll take the rogue on right. He is a bit ripe!
My dear, is yours dead yet? Mine is nearly
There—though having reservations…I think.

VULTURE THE FIRST

Oh, woman, feast! I saw your vast visions
And I heard your swooping song; the high glass.
I saw more…in fact. I saw gluttony
On a level that shames these fat Romans.
And I saw the conclusion—I did.
His late beneficiaries will fall
Before the altar of their next purchase.

VULTURE THE SECOND
I saw that too. Oh, this death-meat is good.

11/10/20

Knowledge of Ages

To walk this world with the knowledge of ages,
Not from genius nor oracular clairvoyance,
Rather a gentle instinct acquired and applied
To view dispassionate the steady future glass.

To know there is no answer to the questions cold,
Though steaming they boil on an unwelcome stove.
Lit by a fool's fool recalling a cauldron cast
In the image of a wizard or statesman smooth.

The downtrodden forever scorned for struggling stuck.
The respectable honored for their eternal luck.

Will it always be so…?

Yeah, I'd say probably.

2/11/20

When the Grave Ceases to be a Portal

When the grave ceases to be a portal,
The threshold to a conjugal paradise,
But instead is a bottomless stairwell
To an infinite oblivion black...
If nothingness conquers loneliness,
And our forms entwined only temporal,
Then I submit to turning time tyrannical.
And will disappear into the limbs and lips
Of this romantic interest.
The sole remnant of my prior beliefs...
And these poems...
...I leave to you in desperation.

12/10/19

Parting After Hurricane Harvey

I.
I knew that you would go
When the brown rivers brash,
Tired of their tantrums
Withdrew their spoilt tears—
The media having moved on
To yet another melodrama…

I knew that you would go,
The pull of twenty years
Against the inertia,
The crisis of mid-stream;
Your frail mount sent overboard,
To drown in the fire of irony?

II.
Before your false return and after your pure departure,
Even the presence of common place things projected
rejection:

A silk tie drooping from a closet door,
A pair of slacks draped from a lonely chair
like a muddy saddle upon the bank.

III.

We will meet again, years hence perhaps,
At a dying mall or teeming concert hall…
You will be coming and I will be going.
We will pause to say hello and confirm
That both are fine, and the unkind years' kind.
You will be sipping wine, and me…stale beer.

9/17

Chimney Chapel

There were
A brood of baby birds
Caught in my chimney,
And knowing what I know of life
I wondered if I
Should not spare them the agony of flight.

But the simple smell of wood smoke
Would rifle the task
Shoot with black clarity
Northward my liberation.
  But the thought
  Of their brittle branches in panic
  Brought my blast to gray
  And that sudden nostalgia for day
  Pelted me with selfish sympathy.

Catching a tan
Decaying with friends
Secretly I awaited their mother.

  But she never came.

Come the waste and grime
Of the holiday season
I swept fossils away wondering…

Wondering if Grace was not merely indifference
Speckled by an occasional fine feather
That catches the every change in the weather
With the same star.

1994

Driving FM 1161 to Work

Memory discriminates through long time.
The precious and the rare monopolize
The mind's space, crowding out life's mad routine.
But mind rebels...or is it something else?
Something our steel and cloud despise like flesh,
Sentiment that cannot shed like dead skin,
But flushes ripe in its own kind of cloud?

For me, it was and is long enduring:
The country mornings, ripe in their own right,
Like an orange crushed in the solar sky.
And whether fallow or sprung, the long road
Sucking me towards the city, past combines
I'd curse like wild hogs or unshackled
Steers, was enough to unman the city's hold.

9/30/20

Before Their Time

Before their time, flaming words were loosed.
Like golden wings they launched into the sky.
But below, the darkness dwelled absolute.
The light revealing ugly naked souls.

Before their time legs strong would wander
    far;
Wander righteous into a Satan's den.
Ideas devoured there would sickly twist.
Misunderstood pearls, the droppings of death.

The exalting throat grew raspy from defeat.
The interrupted darkness, a foot note.
The legs, tiring too soon, soon shrank,
And the bones grew brittle before their time.

2012

Muse Arcane
(with apologies to Keats and Graves)

I.

With words like diamonds fastened fine,
Ordered in a sketchbook divine,
I wandered lost a haunted wood,
Old enough to question if I should.

II.

No means urban would dare lumen,
Only what stars the clouds allowed.
As soggy darkness set, — 'what woman?'
I sought rest on a bough that bowed.

A howl I heard from the thicket thick.
The cry alit my words a wick:
Enflaming from a feeble need,
I rose and pushed through stagnant weed.

III.

Rising in decibels, and high,
The moon now shimmering unclothed,
From behind a tree, a pale thigh…
In poised crescent, unsheathed from robe.

I fast darted for the glimmer,
But what I found was no tremor.
Only the bark of an old oak;
The dirt beneath silken-soaked.

IV.
The howling cry morphed to low moan.
An arm flashed here, and a blond lock there...
Deeper I dared till no light shown,
And all had vanished, asking, 'where?'

A flame appeared like a serpent,
Insisting I kneel and repent.
From what transgression, I knew not.
Within my mouth I tasted rot.

V.
My face half-lit, I cowered there.
As striking as the blades of fire,
From behind an oak she areared,
"Worthy Art Thou to be a Sire?"

Sketchbook in hand she read in turn,
Till tears seared her features learned.
Folding the boards she pointed towards
A bed of petals and silver sword.

VI.
She rode with manic devotion,
Till moonlight foamed and silver laved.
Her face changed with emotion:
And only salvation she waived?

Reciprocal penetration:
An edge drew my pink intestine,
Coiled like a snake, tip to hilt.
The petals frayed, her face did wilt.

VII.
With words like diamonds fastened fine,
Ordered in a sketchbook divine,
I wandered found a haunted wood,
Old enough to question if I should.

12/21/18

An Autumn Morning on the Coastal Plains

Morning mist erases the horizon.
The crests of trees rise
from the milky haze.
The odor of cow shit sticks on the dew.
Geese, in formation,
arrow-through the sky.

A coy coyote shows then vanishes.
Green grass, in the
warming foreground, glistens.
The odor of cow shit sticks on the dew.
The wet sun rises to reclaim itself.

10/09

Watering Hole

On the western edge of our property
There sags, like a marsh primeval,
A depression.
A wild orchard of pecans,
In the last century or so,
Has sprouted about the rim.

All forms of life, excluding human,
Gather at its brim.
Indeed, the health of the tract
Is wholly contingent upon its contents.

In summer, when draught drinks it dry,
Creatures disperse.
Snakes seem to gravitate
Towards the small house
Situated on a subtle hill…

An action we both will regret.

6/10

The Knife You Repeatedly Plunge Into Me

The knife you repeatedly plunge into me
Does not wear with each rapid sweep,
But more precise in its execution.
A strategist, you practice your craft.
But this craft you practice in the dark,
A heretic over a boiling pot.
Stirring your schemes and fastened angles,
Manipulating light, sharpening spells.
A willing subject I have been to your wand,
A devoted doughboy charging the trench.
An unquestioning patriot of love:
Timelessly wounded, but charging still.

The knife you repeatedly plunge into me…
Like a banner, to conquer or to free?

2007

The Return of the Anachronism
(a Southern Gothic)

Up from the rich rows of the once green vine,
To the firm house his late father had raised.
Ragged, like a minstrel, off the front line.
A traitor or a patriot praised?

The plundered home still in the charred twilight.
The last dull daggers of day almost sheathed.
In well-filed flanks the shadows drew night.
He ran his tongue across his hungry teeth.

The summer bugs roared from the fallow field.
The darkness sat as languid as a cow.
He made a table of the family shield;
Nibbled hard bread, wishing it a sow.

Defeat had fallen,
      like an overdue autumn.
From his coat he pulled a flask of laudanum.

5/07

In Search of Mother Earth

With the plague of returning flesh
The sickness of brother's blood
Running thick across his sharpened soul
Cain left the teeming thighs
The now fallen fossil forest
The once ragging chest of wild children
And poetic nakedness.
And roaming landscapes comparatively barren
With dry throat
Cracked lips bleeding regret
Upon a twig
He tied a ragged cloth
A ragged cloth of conquering color
And piercing the unconditional soil
Hoisted and gave birth to a great nation
And longing the blood stuffed arms of understanding
Called the merciless mud
"MOTHER."

1992

To the Lawmakers

Go ahead, rage against your artlessness from the podium,
Swinging at posterity.
Angry because that, after God, only art is immortal?
For your schemes, deals, trickery, bullying and compromise
Are but a trickling hose at the trunk of a drought thirsty,
  Giant tree.

Yes, you may witness a bud or two, but prematurely
The leaf will yellow.
From your artlessness nothing artful can you craft from decay.
The Eye of the world, that will not gaze on you, you have blinded.
A morass of vacancy you will impart; sucking into its vortex…
  Nothingness.

5/15

Medievaling of the Mind

The cosmos is comprised of contraries:
Fire and ice, dark and light, suns and black holes.
Consent is as brief as an estuary.
Twilight and dawn to greater forces fold.
Our white pillars long stained have lost their
    shine.
To a sales pitch the promise decayed.
The Earth reclaims always the boundary line:
Once grand courts of Law, now covered in clay.
For the Darkness, like the Devil, comes to
    collect.
(As the promise in Death usurps sweet life.)
A thousand years—just enough to regret?—
The freedom we squandered for sect and strife.

Humanism gave them milk and honey,
And though fat and full, still they were hungry.

2007

A Live Oak Leaning

Perhaps a hurricane sent it stretching,
Some age before engines echoed about;
Filling field and forest with song-less work,
When natives pensive paused, listening for lore?

From sandy loam reaching, amid Pecans,
Its mass squatted at forty-five degrees;
Standing sentinel for two centuries,
Battling Oak Wilt and wood-boring bugs.
Now, no eager ear in search of song,
The discolored bark and leathery leaves,
Finds enraptured - merely a creased blue print.
Its grim elder stance no match…against progress.

9/09

The Futility and the Torment
(with apologies to The Bard.)

It dawns on one, one day: a paltry fit:
The pointlessness cold of every hot breath.
The pure foolishness of posterity:
The strewn bones in royal catacombs.

The horror in knowing that a life's
    long love
Will vanish into oblivion black.
The connection lost like an average day
We scarce recall as the days yawn on.

A tower honoring rot, our labors;
A cornerstone to our tomb, each brick laid;
Nothing original to redeem,
Or save us; our lone crumb a ditty-dumb...

12/14

She was a Girl and I was a Fool

She was a girl and I was a fool.
She was flippant and free—and I didn't know
The nature of what glued the world together:
The gristle'd seams where nothing green can grow.

She was a girl and I was a child.
Both as righteous as a rain-muscled creek,
That swept us along faster than we knew:
Months like years, days as long as summer weeks.

She was a girl and I was a wound—
She realized finally she'd never heal—
In crowned Womanhood like an Easter morn
She rose from youth with the ease of a wheel.

She was a girl and I was a fool…
And long since grown up, as I have grown cruel.

08/07

The Cave Painter
(or, The First Artist Exile)

His tribe had cast him out.
His only crime that of…
He had wooed a woman.
Not with gut force or strength,
But with an artist's touch.

She rose not in defense,
But rather cold disgust,
Towards he that set her free.
And over his shoulder saw
Her take that savage arm.

The dawn was cold and frosted.
His brush could plant no seed.
He must come to accept it:
Like the sunset lurking…
With no promise of beckon.

But in her womb guarded…
A fugitive fresh grew.

12/1/18

The Enchanted Run

The lake is as still as a photograph.
The insects of summer swarm the surface.
The decaying Sun leaves his autograph:
Slivers of dancing gold superfluous.

Yes, night is the true reign of the living,
Trumpeting the return of the maiden,
A gauze white gown drags behind her leaving,
Purple passage through blue boughs moss laden.

The brown bayou rabbit, the slow opossum,
We know only of these brutes in-between.
In the twilight or dawn as brief as a blossom,
Reconnaissance for the chorus unseen.

Sleep you tired people,
    dream if you can…
Of the garden deep from which you were banned.

2006

A Record of Suffering?

I.
Was there a record of his suffering,
Anywhere other than his beating breast?
Those nights in May vanished in a blink;
Those ripe breasts like a butterfly spread;
His body above in the light-lined dark.
Ignorant that the door was closing quick,
The beams of spring severed too soon.

II.
Stranded in a summer robbed of its radiance,
Starting in September, he stood apart.
In the white light that was always yellowing,
He stamped the page with a voice like a fist.
But the musky scent of old books envious
Of blood and flesh, would claim the frail lungs.
The health of summer severed too soon.

III.
In the bent shadows a shadow bent
Finds its way crooked under thin accolades:
Leaves garlanding an early waiting winter:
Insignificance tugging from the chasm.
Whether much or little it matters not,
The whole of it in the end just a hole;
Its singular worth simply worthless.

IV.
   Was there a record of his suffering?
   Anywhere other than his bleeding breast?
   Yes; but none so as telling...

   ...None.

5/16

Nuper Romanus

He seized her by the waist, thrusting her forward.
Her soft naked breasts, hard within his chest.
Her starved neck dangled, an angle acute.
The hushed lips pursed like a long open rose.

Their kiss betraying the impulse of the age...

The bed posts cracked, like the threshold's columns.
The plush violet sheets, far too long a plain.
Though her dampness inviting...not her womb...
The seed of structure stopped, by season frozen.

As she whispered... "far too late, my love...
        ...far, far too late."

2/18

Fangs of Discontent

The predisposition to discontent
Harangues like a trained, vicious police dog.
We cower and cover, cupping our privates;
Faith in the security of the bite.

What breeds sequestered in the cellular
Cell, that unlocks the need for imprisonment?
Does gorging till sickness feed emptiness?
The sloppy trough a distraction from the cage?

What nut would conjure a mirage of goods
To satiate the masses with vomit?
What plot sinister trade the future fat,
For the ribcage of everlasting debt?

The throat is thy shrine...
Fangs of Discontent.
By rote we shall find,
Life is 'The Lament'.

More...more...evermore...

Hands idle at the keyboard will condemn
Appendages guiding the intellect:
The irony of accessibility;
Ignorance elect, void of circumstance.

Fangs of Discontent
Clench this mortal clay.
Drain our Godless life,
That sucks anyway.

4/15/20

Masks

Four hundred years ago, or four-thousand—
What's the difference really—?
There are still slanted roofs and walls.
There are still hallways and doors;
Still cooking utensils and cups.
On the outside…? still distending roads.
And whether paved or no
Are nonetheless roads.

And still masks…
Some of which never needed hooks—
And still don't—to hang upon.

And still those fooled by their
Persuasive traits and numbing charms.
Yes, still those square, stealing smiles,
Whether by design or disguise,
Angling away the wheels of escape.

1/5/21

Is Our Lovemaking a Confessional?

Is our lovemaking a confessional?
You asked me, your head perched on your pillow.
Your creased sheets a pallet of entrails;
Or its thread rifts a trail towards Calvary?

What can I say to you, lying naked?
Does not my nakedness speak for itself?
I am both your green bard sacrificial,
As well as the cursed judge of Judea.

If one exile cannot confide his thoughts,
Plant their futility in the quiet womb
Of his fellow exile; what use this life?
What use this nothingness bereft the void?

If our lovemaking is a confessional,
Then I confess: I confess to its need.
My self-regard absolute; but not so:
Its one flaw, the need of an ear pious.

1/14

Irony and Symbolism 101

The image rises in the mind still—
As if the mere selling of it would
Appease its demand on the imagination.
Most often at night, in dreams awkward
As the crutch to a fresh cripple's under arm,
I emerge upon the stilted face raised
By my late father. The fat, fluted columns,
Long ago erected, would support more
Than merely the white, obtuse pediment
That angled oppressively down on
A young, rebellious youth who sought
To betray it.
Far from Yeat's "Tower," or even Simms',
Woodlawn, still this chalk edifice
Scribed something indelible on my mind.
The old man must rest utterly satisfied,
To think his practical sense would impart,
A primeval art I could never raze.

1/10

It is a Barren Spring

It is a barren spring
That which returns, returns.
But that which does not
Somehow diminishes that
Which does.

Damage prevails.
Scars reveal themselves.
The drought has both penetrated,
And reached up from the grave:

A Systemic sickness,
A Lineage of Loss.

Long rains profuse
Hasten the rot.

4/12

Southron Sage (for W.G. Simms)

Like the tree felled to publish the poem
That sings of its majesty eternal,
So your heart was Cauldron born, thus joined
Those that distill life from a kernel.

It's true that the empty numeral claimed your age
And that hemlock stained your lie searing lip.
And though a condemned shadow,
  the Southern sage,
From your mossy bark never could you slip.

To strain from the earth, no better place:
Your inherited crow's feet were furrows
That channeled the tears of your run-down race;
Those forbidden to build…denied a tomorrow.

If your age ended as a cage and little else,
Better you were a prisoner of place than of self.

2009

*Southron (South-ron): Chiefly Southern.

Her Cries Upon Climax

Her cries upon climax,
He could not recollect.
He recalled a sound, but could not,
For the life of him,
Remember the tone...
    The timbre...
    The anima...
He prayed that, upon blessed death,
Her lone muse would revisit,
Whispering those fateful notes.
Those shapes in air, read by an ear.

11/12

On the Failure of U.S. Presidents
from the New South

Currently condemned cradle of a country factioned.
Agrarian patriarchs with everything to lose:
Washington, Jefferson, Monroe, Jackson!
Self-Actualization of the ordainment to choose.
Transplanted planters, gallants bearing arms:
Heraldic thread woven in umber American earth.
Patriots or traitors to acrimonious alarm!
Rationalism's revolt: Romanticism's worth.
The tradition stands disseminated two centuries later:
Johnson, Carter, Clinton and Bush.
Persuasion is not principle, nor obstinacy character—
From Lettered Statesman to flaccid mush.

   From an age of forward fire, the oldest living revolution,
Sacked by Sons Southern: From destiny to destitution.

2007

Multiculturalism vs. The Melting Pot

The hepatitis of a nation's lair.
The puzzle utterly unsolvable.
Pioneer wagon of stone wheels
    square.
Pieces and foreign parts unworkable.

Fat cauldron steaming of blood, spit and
    glue.
Tongues sharp or wide, stirred with an Anglo stick.
Soul churned into soles for strong working shoes.
The excess cast for beams and climbing brick.

A nation without a voice is a nation not,
But a series of fragments unlocking.
Pride alone prefers a purebred to mutt.
It's hell, livid Cerberus guards barking.

Shatter the pot, break the rod if you will,
Do not later cry when the heart is still.

2008

Regeneratus

Acres burned this past Fall
Have found root, stifling
The charred scent so obtuse.
"That widda Ellington
Will think twice before she
Burns her brush in a drought!"

Stalled under the Live Oak,
An oil leak dripped down
From the pan for a year
Sapping the fledgling till
Leaves turned slowly to brown.
"Post-moltin', green she were!"

Winter was hard this year
"A stove was all we had."
Window-units were down
"Stove was all that we had!"
Cold like a phantom crept
Under floorboards and sheets.

"The heat ain't so bad here
We can sit and watch the
Sun sinking through slow June."
The hum of cattle-cars
Barely breaks the silence.
Dense sleep blankets the farms.

2009

There is a Woman with an Ancient Soul

There is a woman
With an ancient soul
Kindred to mine I do not know,
But a soul…
A soul with an embrace
Like a Spartan room
Near a window with which
To gaze at the world
And all its dead, its dying,
Living and yet unborn blossoms.
Chair and desk to reflect
Pen and paper to predict.
A well-fed place of peace:
The fulcrum of Beauty's lore
Not entirely detached
From the rugged grip
Of day to day doings.
A fertile field that all men must find
And so very few ever do.

There is a woman
With an ancient soul…
And I have found her.

1996

A Minor Poet

His failed youth was filled
With exalted imitations.
Silly love poems given to fickle
Beauties largely undeserving.
And there were songs too,
More real than the ink nightingales
He proudly penned, but affected nonetheless.

They got him nowhere.

So completely nowhere, that by twenty-five,
He could, from the bottom of his bitter heart,
Proclaim with indignant disgust
That *he*, did not believe in Love.

Love was the epitome of immaturity.
A cheesy greeting card decorated with homespun flowers
And some corny rhyme reminiscent of the
Embarrassing slop he used to pander.

Then, he met her.

(Well, he didn't just meet her,
He had known her for years.)

Which made it worse,

For she could recall
With impartial envy
The days when even the slightest smile
Would send him spinning.

But now…with her, nothing.

He, being the dazed creature that he was,
Could not understand that the audience
Rarely hears the clearing of the throat
The slight slip in pitch.

What seemed so brazenly flat to him
Was, because of its obvious sincerity
Full of bright clarity for her.

It was too late.

The technical prowess of the man
Lacked the raw temper of the child.

His labors were exactly that, labors.

All that he was left with
Composition after composition
Was denial.

(Having ventured into some dark fresh digression)

A crumpled page on the floor
Beside the coffee table...

No stunning description,
No Zhivago-like subtlety...

Only the words...

I LOVE YOU.

1998

The Age of Greatness

The Age of Greatness has passed. What remains is the age
  of mediocrity.
  Maybe the mad philosopher was right:
Democracy leads to the decay of those ordained to carry
The original torch, kept lit through time, of all that makes
  life worth living for.

The only endeavor that can survive intact, without
  amendment,
  With the exception of simple math and war—
Science, technology, engineering, are transient and
  changing…
We can honor them for their innovation, but they are a
  footnote to the present—

…Only Art is eternal, whether ten thousand years old or
  ten hours.

5/12/21

Relativity of Marching

Marching up Mt. Bonnell in the weekend April air—
The granite steps soiled from too many tourists;
The infinite sky as blue as the Aegean deep—
I could feel the lungs pulling air into the blood stream,
And the heart pumping victorious like a thoroughbred.
Along the way I would need to navigate the short
Of breath and plain out of shape.
But once atop, the burning legs relaxed
And the oxygen evened out the spastic diaphragm.
And what I beheld was a three-layered vista:
The Colorado below; unopposed atmosphere above;
Between: the curves of green studded hills.
And though the hills were cancerous with too many houses
Still it was a climb worth the climbing.

Monday morning I returned to the Capitol restored.
Duty inclined me to run some information up to
The House floor. Steps…many many steps.
When I reached the pit outside the chamber
And summated the collection of reputations…
…I had to pause for dearth of breath.

5/17/21

The Last Poet

The last poet will never be read
By anyone anywhere
For a thousand years at least.

The last poet's beauty
Will be an ugly affront
To the silent raiders

The sudden swarms of pretentious
Those flat inheritors
The fabled meek.

For the womb is empty
Decay has no eye for the ordained
Only loathsome reward
For its suicidal cohorts in genocide.

The last poet will feel the terrible pangs
Of all the atrocities ever at once.
Ever since individuals,
To the extreme dismay and protest of their peers,
Straightened up, walked upright.

The last poet will have no market
History is his rejection slip.

His predecessors possessed the future
They had the vision
The last poet possesses only the sight:
  Hindsight
He knows he is standing at the threshold

Behind him the dream of redemption
Before him inevitable oblivion.

The last poet will die an old man
Miserable, the last of his race
Without even the trick of eternity
To comfort his distance.

The last poet is alive and writing as I rave.

1996

Verse Log of the 87th

ON THE EVE OF THE 87TH
TEXAS STATE LEGISLATURE (Austin)

I can't now know why, I viewed this dome romantically.
In our lifetimes, stripped of meaning,
Can we not find sustenance in our lives together?
Victuals to replace the lies
Total that load the table weighted with absorption.

All I want now is to come home to you:
Your dogs, garden, luxuriant hair.
Sometimes I wish the old wounds would rebel,
Sidelining me, so I can at last stop.
But then I worry, you may not want me… anymore.

1/11/21

INAUGURATION WEEK IN DC (Austin)

Capitol empty.
Only Jackson and I.
Legislators sent home.
I cut junior staff loose
To cover my ass,
As there have been reports
of possible terror attacks.
Told Jackson it was his choice.
He chose to brave it.

Walking the silent halls,
my sole convoy the soles
of my boots on the mosaic tiles,
I find door after door, floor after floor
locked and hollow. Only state
troopers, stationed strategically,
Confirm that I am not in purgatory.
It is both peaceful and creepy.
Troopers are stoic unless greeted,
But are eager to say 'hello.'

I stop by the pisser on my
way back to base. I've washed my
hands so many times they bleed.

1/19-20/21

SUNDAY MORNING 10AM
(Sandra's garden, Houston)

Words are the tools of poets;
Playthings for lawmakers and lawyers.
This seems upside down, I think.
But one is alchemy, the other…Irons.

My father once said, '*If lawyers are so*
goddamned smart, then there wouldn't
be so fuckin' many of 'em,'

This is true…
But rot makes for a potent alchemy
…and alliance.

1/24/21

LEAVING SANDRA'S FOR AUSTIN
(on the road)

All weekend was a
Soggy grey quilt sagging
Over the city. Monday:
Rushing as I do, disturbs
Sandra's equilibrium—
(She is, was, and eternally beautiful).
Skipped the dog walk,
thus consolation?
Running late. Far to go.
I'd rather trace the tree-lined streets
of quaint Lazy Brook than race
to the Capitol. But duty calls.
(Road construction – I10)
Long way around the barn:
Take 290 to Bastrop
Pines stand guard all through
Hwy 21, as if pine nettles
have knitted safe green passage.
Poor Bastrop proper,
once a quaint nook itself,
now a traffic jam.
It's the tragedy of Texas
writ small.

Once in Austin the gut sinks.
The day's duties diminish
the majesty of the hills.
Finally at the Cap.

Staff suited up and
ready for battle.
But there is no map.

1/25/21

BALANCE?

Left Sandra's on Monday morning,
and went straight to the Capitol.
(It was a good weekend as she
took me to see the Hotel ZaZa
in the Museum District in Houston.
It was her idea, as I had texted her the week
prior for a cool hotel in H-town:
(Reconnaissance for my next novel.)

The Cap was quiet and heavily armed.
I got back to my apartment after an absence
of three days. Same shithole I'd left
on Friday morning. Tuesday morning the
toilet struggles to flush. I'm concerned.
I don't want to get worried. Worried is bad.
Life is weird, really weird. It gives and takes
away—then gives more…and in places one
would never expect (Biblical wisdom).
For me, this session…it's traffic.
The pandemic has a boon, I get to work in
less than fifteen minutes. But life is balance:
The traffic doesn't back up…but maybe
Something else will?

Covid scare this week.
An intern tested positive,
the rest of us negative.
Though he's fine I'll be short
on staff for at least another week.
Negative is good I think,
it's the only position or disposition
or diagnosis that makes any
circular sense in this boxed-in
world of ours.
Milton you were right...maybe?
If *the mind is its own place*
Then I will quarter myself
in a domain with no sharp angles
...always arriving at a healthy doubt.

The eyes weaken and go bad.
The skin rebels against the chin,
defecting to the camp of gravity.
(Newton was politically coy.)
But I have my guys, my staff.
And like Thomas Becket
I have surrounded myself with
a coterie of young urban scholars,
(some not so urbane, or scholarly).
It does not matter. They are a good crew,
And I get to feign that somehow
I am imparting a crumb of value.
Today (Saturday) the weather was
immaculate. Perfect. And if rumored
Heaven be something more than
A fanatical blaze or social gossip…
Then it must have given a small hint
today when it chose to herald the sky.

End of week 2/1

OBSERVATIONS BEFORE THE STORM

It's both funny and unsettling
to watch the interns intent interest
at the ceremonial aspect of the
House floor. We waste so much
time here. It's truly ridiculous.
So many problems. So much to do.
I have no time for political pomp.
No time for the purple stage.
Elect me and let me do your work.
But the play goes on in perpetuity.
And I am convinced that as long
as the populace salivates over
Simple wasteful distracting shadows…
the people will serve the servants.

Forgot to mention we got committee assignments last
Thursday. Pensions, Investments and Financial Services,
and County Affairs.

Metaphor of the moment:

The ship has hit the iceberg.
The hull is taking on water.
Texas has the best life boat.
Instead of an act of survival,
our leaders take inventory
of the accouterments on deck.

Dropped into Waterloo Records on North Lamar
on Wednesday. Had nothing particular I was mining
but they were finally open for in-store shopping.
Felt obligated to make a purchase, so I grabbed some
music and a movie. At check out I asked the cashier
how business was doing—were they surviving?
Gus (guy's name) and I then discussed the death of Austin.
He is a native and probably in his late thirties
or early forties. Waterloo will ultimately be
devoured by the jaws of consumer capitalism,
as a developer has purchased the property and has
plans for a high-dollar high-rise. Everything that made
this town a town is rapidly vanishing. What is left
is the worst of the world.

News of the a coming winter blast
shove away all other concerns.
I'm on the first floor of a two-story
complex. Decide to meet the ruckus
above. Two women, very inviting.
I inform them of my departure in the morning.
Please, please keep your taps pouring.
They welcome me in and we drink for hours.

Made it back to Sandra's on Friday with presents
and roses (six red, six white). Valentine's dinner on Saturday.
It was a heartwarming evening and not at all a portent
of what gift the Artic had ready to deliver.

End of week 2/8

LIFE IN THE FROZEN LANE

Sunday: prepared for Uri.
Do we really need to name winter storms?
After this thing…Yes! It's like a fuckin' hurricane.
Sandra and I constructed a canopy
for the lemon tree off her back patio.
Drink then sleep.

Monday: drank too much Sunday night.
Passed out after watching Colombo.
Wake up to find the kitchen tap is mute.
Shit! we forgot to keep the faucets dripping.

Tuesday forward: ice sparkles and shatters like glass.
Dripping faucets carry on conversations.
Electricity is a commodity more valuable
than gold or insider trading info.
Water is water: Both life bestowing
and equally destructive. Frozen pipes
are the lawmakers now; anxiety the judge.

Rolling black outs after 8 hrs. of nothing.
Nothingness is powerful. And Darkness his bride,
as the ancients well knew, gives birth to Cold.
They are the Power Couple of the moment.

(Now I know why all these assholes move down here.)

Frig no longer cold.
Worried about food.
Dig up snow and ice.
Move contents of frig
to coolers outside.
We find the pool has a
winter use: flushing toilets!

Breakfast upset my stomach.
Worried about dinner.
At least I found gas
to fill up my car.
Night comes.
Candles are timeless.

A new word for public consumption: not Uri, but ERCOT.

End of week 2/14

Scavenge for food and water Sunday morning,
after a Saturday of struggle and communication
breakdown between Sandra and I.
I head back to ATX.
Worried about the pipes in my apt—
anxiety the entirety of the trip.
Find everything intact and dry.
I'm exhausted. Wit fails me.
The pen is empty.

Capitol is dull compared to the outside world:
Nothing going on, but a fire alarm late Monday.
No fire apparently. Stood outside and sweated
…in a suit.

Thursday: Joint Committee Hearing to address
the Uri blackout. Goes on all day and into the night.
Drinking beer and enjoying pizza at the office.
ERCOT has their shit together.

Later that night I have a phone call with Sandra.
Though the cold is gone it stubbornly stays.
We are on a relationship sabbatical.
That may be an oxymoron.

End of week of 2/21

LIFE RESUMES

Sunday morning I rise low and hungover.
The sabbatical is over. We are still in love.

Monday I'm stuck on a conference call
with the Chronic Kidney Disease Task Force,
first thing. Is ignorance a chronic disease?
I'm speaking of myself of course.

Later that night Sandra and I have a heart-to-heart.
It's good.

Tuesday: The masks will be off soon.
      Freedom now a craven boon.
      I need a beer, a tune to croon.
      A night on the town, under the moon.

The rest of the week things start moving, however slowly.
Hearing Requests, our first committee hearing, amend-
ments for this or that.

Friday I drive back to Sandra's. Yay!

Saturday afternoon we clear out the dead,
withered remnants from the recent winter storm,
then plant a climbing rose. A reclamation of Life.
Wash up and hit the Houston Museum of Fine Arts
to see a David Hockney exhibit.
He's juxtaposed with Van Gogh. If there's any
connection here I can't really see what it is other than
they both do trees. Hockney's paintings are amateurish,

though his charcoals have some flair.
The digital iPad drawings do nothing for me.
If there's any statement here it's the deterioration
of representational art. (It is better than a lump of concrete.)
That's all I have to say.
Drinks at Under the Volcano.
Dinner at the Raven Grill.

End of week of 2/28

Sunday under a chrome blue sky
The lady and I walk the dogs
and later ride bicycles.
Dinner is pecan crusted chicken.

Back in Austin:
House Pensions hearing Wednesday morning.
Synopsis: state funded public retirement systems are the
Gordian Knot.
Solution: opt out. Let me keep my money, I'll figure it out
on my own.
Better solution: die before you need it.

*(Point worth noting, and nothing to do with anything:
Listening to shit loads of C&W since my initial arrival
In ATX. Not bad country but great country. I do have
impeccable taste. Buying old CD's and DVD's in
preparation of the coming knowledge dump. Books too.)
I'm a cultural prepper.*

End of week of 3/7

HELL WEEK

Sunday at Sandra's was like knowing you're
going to be shipped to Devil's Island in a few hours.
Plus, her garden is gone. The winter robbed the senses
of all abundance. It will grow back, and that which
does not, can be seeded again. I wish I'd gone into
the nursery business.

My anxiety is well founded. My instincts
are razor sharp. But I'm a fucking moron.
Contrarians be damned. I do work in
government for a reason (or lack thereof).

Week in summary: I should have slashed my wrists
upon waking…Just loaded up on coffee and nicotine
and done the whole bloody business. Everything that
could go wrong goes awry. Bills may not make it because
of tiny details a stellar telescope could not see coming.
Anxiety grips the gut; irritation like grit in the eye.
From Monday thru Thursday it's the same slap
in the face. Scramble around scouring for fixes.
Words like, 'unconstitutional', 'germane', and
'Local Bill' fire the razor-sharp explosion.

Thursday afternoon the red-tinted super nova
I'm drowning in…fragmentizes… leaving a hole.
A call from Sandra fills the murky void.
Her voice is like European butter to the blasted
ears. Her news is good. Letting her go is like a
spaceman who realizes the pulling hole is dense
with crushing gravity going forward.

However I'm covered in the butter of her voice.
The blade would probably just slide off.
No profusion of blood or vacuum.

Friday March Madness starts.
Jackson starts drinking at noon.
He is the wisest among us.

Stay in ATX.

End of week of 3/14

THE HUMAN PINBALL

Hell week becomes an official past time.
The problems of the world a spectator sport.
I feel the slinging plunger at my back.
Bumper after bumper, path after path.
He who controls the flippers controls the world.
   This is not me.

Thursday Pensions meeting: Let's move on it!
But where? It's a cluster fuck and I'm expected to
provide the glue. Can there be hope with no
plan? Can there be direction with no compass?

Friday I'm stuck in traffic trying to get to Sandra's.
I finally make it and make a confession about
something that's been bothering me for a month.
(An affliction that will go unnamed—nothing sexual).
She is very kind and understanding. Her sweetness
a proxy to the decimated garden.

Turkey burgers and Colombo on Saturday night!

End of week of 3/21

Sunday it's chilly. I have to leave and go back to ATX.
Somewhat down in the dumps. Sandra encourages me
to risk I10. I do. It works. Back at the apt. in two and a half.

The week goes well in comparison.
Some breakthroughs with a major bill concept.
The Pensions bill appears to have a vehicle.
I reserve further comments for later when more is…
    revealed.

Good crackin' at the chiropractor. Doc's appointment in
the morning for my secret issue.

Not much I can do about the secret issue but wait.
Doc was cool. Take 290 all the way to Sandra's.

Friday night we meet her friend Beth at the Rustic
in Downtown Houston. Beth introduced us.
No plans for a first born, but if there were
I'd owe her all within the swaddling cloth.

Saturday we get a late start. Sleeping in till
10 AM is a gift I take advantage of. Around 3
we decide to take the trip to Winnie to see
the Houston Audubon Sanctuary, at High
Island/Smith Oaks. It's a long trek, and through
one of the ugliest parts of Houston. The day is dreary.
Once at Winnie we take a sharp south
towards Bolivar Peninsula. I have no expectations
and frankly wasn't up for the trip. But Sandra

persisted. And WOW, I'm glad she did.
The overcast day is the perfect setting.
A long, forty foot high plank initiates our journey.
It bends and twists through coastal wilderness
until we arrive at the spectacle:
A series of nesting rooks in a silver lake.
Egrets by the hundreds perform their rituals,
indifferent to the human eyes invading their space.
A series of taut arbors wrap the waters.
I imagine the native Karankawa winding
like cottonmouths through the knotted shaft.
Or, ancient druids in stolid madness moving
towards a site of ceremonial sacrifice.

End of week 3/28

EASTER SUNDAY

We set off on our ritual dog walk, this time
through West 11th St. Park — (a favorite spot).
We skirt the edge of the copse and discover
a tiny, orphaned opossum trembling on a
large root next to an oak. Flies cover its face.
I insist we find a way to rescue it. The smell of death
lingers from the wood. We can only surmise the mother
is dead. Sandra is reticent, not knowing what to do.
She senses my insistence. We leave for our walk
and upon return, the opossum is still present.
We find a wildlife rehabilitation facility near by.
We rush home, grab an empty Amazon box, return,
snatch up the poor little thing and race to the rehab center.
All is glorious on this day of resurrection.
The creature will get a second chance at life.

Feeling calm and vindicated, we pop into a nursery
and purchase a few plants to replenish Sandra's garden.
Dirt under the nails, a nagging back ache and other pains…
I can't think of a better way to spend Easter Sunday.
And I mean it.

INTO THE MADDING CROWD

Monday it's back to ATX. This was most likely
my last weekend at Sandra's until Sine Die.
I will miss her and the fruition of spring.
When I return the sun will have devoured the sky.

Tuesday tears out of the gate with ferocity.
Anxiety over our pensions concept is taking toll.
I am always prepared for disaster. It lowers one's
expectations.

In the afternoon the boss and I meet with the
Speaker's campaign team. It is pointless and they
are contemptuous – knowing nothing of our district.
I mean the guy didn't even know we had a Primary
opponent last year. We leave knowing we have most
likely wasted our time.

At close of day, we still don't have
legal language for our portion of the omnibus.
The hearing is in the morning…

The sun is but a fable when I get to the Capitol.
Our language has arrived. Much scrambling between
offices regarding the layout. Then…it happens…
and…it goes right under the radar. Just like I like it.

Still the verdict is out if our language is germane
to the bill. That is for the House Parliamentarian
to decide…

…and within a few hours (not enough time to analyze)
they come back with a big fuck you – and with no
explanation…just NO! Fresh scrambling resumes…

By Friday I'm wacked out as is everyone else.
Friday is our first Friday calendar. At 1 PM
Jackson and I have to endure a tutorial on the
new redistricting software. Welcome to the new
age, where the application supersedes what it
is intended to do. The thought of the
whole thing (app and redistricting itself)
weighs on me like an albatross around the neck.
Oh, Sam, you were a lucky man to be born when
you were. To be a creature of imagination in this
age of mediocrity is worse than the illusion
shattering guillotine that you and Wordsworth
witnessed. I am an anachronism. I should have
been born in 1790. Instead I'm stuck here with
no instruments to guide.
Art is dead and the can't-doers have control.

Still there are some signs of hope, work wise.
The comptroller's office signs off on some language
I put together for a bill that will be heard on Monday.

I get back to the apartment (I will never call it home)
and finally try to relax. Sandra is in Charleston
living it up. I get a call from the Speaker's guy we met
with on Tuesday. He has bad news…before he met
with us he met with someone who has Covid. He's

calling to let me know we were exposed.
Thanks for letting me know, dude.

Stick around ATX all weekend.

End of week of 4/4

Monday I get to the Cap at 5 AM.

Going through the motions this week.
Similar to a hyena at a slaughter.
Most of our bills are stuck but some are moving.
The Pensions bill should find the floor.
Filling a late bill on Friday. It has to do
with a pilot program for pensions. This
is different from the bill presently moving
through the system, that's a study bill.
(Gets confusing I know.)

On Thor's Day we hear the permitless carry bill.
Once upon a time, in previous sessions, it was
called Constitutional Carry. And never made it
out of committee. The layout on the
floor goes on for some seven hrs. It is contentious.
Much weeping and grand standing. If things
go and come back again, then what wonder
that we find ourselves back in the Wild West.
Is the past any less preferable than the
dystopian future? If Time is a stairwell,
or a plane, either or...all things occur
simultaneously and are acted out without
sequence. We are heaped up upon our heirs
and ancestors. The apes are never far and
weigh more than we do. It passes...

Then it passes third reading on Friday—
On its way to the Senate!
Our Late Bill request gets unanimous
permission from the House. We have
a bill! Much is riding on this. The chances
of it surviving the process are as lean
as a stray dog. My job will be to find
someone with a willing bowl to place
out in the vast, unceasing darkness that
envelopes the protruding ribcage that
no one wants to see.

Waterloo Records after work. I've been
listening to Fleetwood Mac a lot.

ATX again this weekend—No Sandra.

*Note: Not sure if I've mentioned this yet.
I've had little sleep and my mind is mush.
I've been working on my fifth novel since
I got up to Austin. Churned out some ten
chapters in two months. My churning has
turned into a trickle. Trying to keep it up,
but it's getting harder and harder.*

End of week 4/11

Head out to the Ranch on Sunday morning
to check up on the place and do laundry.
Grab a couple of McMurtry novels for Sandra.
I gave her Cadillac Jack and All My Friends…
for Valentine's Day. He died not too long afterward,
so now she's hooked. A dead bard is an eternal one.

The plumbing works! Head home that afternoon.
(Think I failed to mention my pipes broke at the Ranch.)

(Disclaimer: I'm writing this a week
later so it's all a bit fuzzy, so I'm going to summarize):
Hearings this week in Land and Resource Mgmt
and Natural Resources (LRM; NR). We also have
bills being voted out of committee and those that
have been voted out. I'm rushing around the Capitol
trying to determine their status, persuading clerks
to move in our favor, and hunting Senate Sponsors.
I'm on a roll, in fact I'm kicking proverbial ass.
Until…let me back up…OK, so we have the NR
Hearing for what we call the TCEQ Notification
Bill (Tx Commission on Environmental Quality).
It fucking breaks down to just a few phone calls
made by the commission to inform cities that
they have brain-eating amoebas in their water.
TCEQ is trying to kill it because they can't understand.
I get the votes, meaning all nine on the NR committee
will vote for it to get it out of committee.

So I strut up from underground to Ground Level.
I'm feeling good, as I'm getting bills on the Calendar
and snagging Senate Sponsors. I walk in with a
check card full of checks. I mean, I'm delivering
the head of the enemy of the people. I might as well
be traversing the Acropolis towards the Temple
of Athena. I walk through the door, head over to the
clerk's desk, and drop the card on his desk like it's
a severed head with hair of serpents. I have the votes!
No. What if I have a problem with it? Uh…but none
of the committee members have a problem. But TCEQ
has a problem with it. Do we work for TCEQ or for the
PEOPLE OF TEXAS? And remember, I just brought
you the head of the enemy of the people!

This is not the end of this. It will continue.
But on to Budget Night…

Thursday is Budget Night. The first true
Intra-office party night at the Capitol.
We have plenty of booze and catered food.
Staff, the carnivorous fiends that they are,
are gorging themselves at the expensive trough.
We are all geared up for a long fight and a long night.
It starts off as we expected: Points of Order…Points
Of Order…Points Of Order…get the picture?
We're going to be here till sunrise tomorrow.
Some staffers are drinking by 3 PM. I'm more
conservative: No booze until 6. So we start—
and slow! Staffers get restless as dark approaches,
mingling from office to office. I have a great

conversation with a staffer from another office
about the end of Western Civilization.
But wait! Maybe we're not all doomed!
By 10:30 it's done! What now? The consensus?
The Cloak Room awaits…
Down the sandy limestone steps and into
the Cauldron of the Capitol. The place is packed.
A true super-spreader. We get our drinks and
squeeze into a corner. The cantankerous clerk
is present. He's headed up to have a smoke, and
I follow. We bond under a cloud of monoxide.
At least he's shooting me straight. We can work this out.

Friday I'm apprehensive, as Sandra's making her
first visit to see me up in ATX. Under a panoply
of drizzle she arrives, meets staff and then I take
her through the Legislative Reference Library, which
houses three of my books. We then trek the Capitol for
a bit. She's in love with architecture.
We get back to my apt. and she is not totally disgusted.
That night we meet a colleague of mine who just so
happens to be the younger brother of Beth, the woman
who introduced us.

Saturday we sleep in and enjoy a late breakfast.
We're off into a sterling day climbing Mt. Bonnell,
then dinner with an old friend of mine who is an
abject introvert. Sandra does a great job of getting
him out of his shell.

End of week of 4/18

Sandra has a talent for finding the grand alcoves
of life. Sunday, before she departs back for Houston,
we take a tour of the Umlauf Sculpture Garden and
Museum. She loves much of modern sculpture.
I can appreciate some of it but it doesn't really
speak to me. Umlauf speaks to me, not only because
his pieces are representational, but because they are
potent. He taught at UT at one point and I find
that odd now. Many of his sculptures have a
Christian theme. No more need be said.

We get a smoothie and then she's on her way.
I'm a little sad.

But no time for sadness or happiness or anything else
remotely human.

Monday it's back to the arena and the back stabbing.
TCEQ will get its way and we will defer to their
version of our NR bill to get it out of committee.
(I guess I need to work on my bonding.)
But it is a game we are playing. We will fuck them
in the Senate with the same blade they have us.

Tuesday I'm consumed with the late bill, as
it will be heard in Pensions on Wednesday.
A late afternoon meeting with ERS goes...
well...not very well. The executive director
wants no part of it even though his construct
is mangled and dying.

The hearing goes well on Wednesday morning.
Left Pending.

In-between all of this are countless fast balls,
flying daggers, and invisible bullets that make up
a general day at this point in session.

Thursday is a shit show of controversial bills.
Goes on and on. Thursday night an intense pain
settles into my low back and hip.
Friday the same, both endless floor acrobats
and hip pain. I'm trying to get out of ATX to
go to Sandra's as the Kentucky Derby is Saturday.
I can barely walk by the end of the day and the
weather is going to hell. I call Sandra and tell
her I'll be there in the morning…
Saturday morning is catastrophe.
Extreme dizziness and vertigo.
Blood Pressure is 192/119.
I need to go to ER. Won't go.
If the heart doesn't kill me
the bills will. I languish all day.
Try to make the trip in the lashing
rain. Only make it a few miles.
Sandra is a saint and understanding.
I return back to my apt in defeat.

End of week of 4/25

Sunday I feel better and get out and about.
The sterling sky soothes the aching heart.
But it won't last.

Monday the heart fever is back and my
BP is as nearly as high as it was on Saturday.
I have to have a staffer squeeze my car into
my assigned space. I take a trip to the House
nurse and she is so alarmed that she refers me
to an Austin doctor who is kind enough to get
me in at a moment's notice. He is very cool, an
actual human being.
The diagnosis: I need to learn to manage stress.
A poem unworkable.

*(Note: I have been derelict in my log. I have
yet to mention Daveed, a staffer. Daveed is
David, as he is Hispanic we call him Daveed.
Daveed is one of the best people I have ever
known. He is kind, jovial, and has the best attitude.
He is young (twenty-one), and I pray that the world does
not rip away that which is best in him.)*

As the week unravels the BP is still an issue,
but I'm keeping on. It's hard because I'm running
around with amendments for this or that in emergency
mode. Everything at this point is an emergency.

Wednesday my health breaks for the better as does the
weather outside. Upon waking I have a moment

of clarity, or a revelation of sorts. I've been rereading
Robinson Jeffers and his arcane philosophy of life.
Jeffers breaks down all existence and experience,
whether human or not, animate or inanimate,
to the simple cycle of all creation. If you're
looking for answers, there's the Bible. If you're
not, then there is reprieve from the anxiety of
being. You are not that important.

I feel decent as I zoom off to work.

More bat shit bills on the floor, and even more
bills that no one really understands but somehow
pass. This is the beginning of a long stint of
gruesomeness. Watching the House floor
should be required study in school. It will
discourage the youthful inclination towards
utopianism. It is a lesson in leadership. And
what happens when psychopaths congregate.

The big one Wednesday is the Heartbeat Bill.
Whatever one may think about abortion it must
be stated that the layout of the bill was terrible.
The Republicans could have put a cardboard box
at the front mic and the bill would have passed.

The lawyers vomit tangled technicalities for hours
and then the emotionalism inevitably begins. This
goes on until 1 AM.

Thursday is another long day. The anti-defund the police
bill draws out for some four hrs. The Elections bill, another
poor layout, agonizes on till 3 AM, until it is finally put
out of its misery by adopting all the amendments.
There are nearly 150.

Back by 9 in the morning. Fuck me. But I'm
leaving for Sandra's at some point. I haven't
been back to her home in five weeks.

Saturday Jackson holds down the fort as the
House is on the floor. I'm in Houston sleeping.

For Mother's Day Sandra goes solo to meet her
mom. I'm full of aches and pains so I can't go
to the gym. Instead I take a mystical stroll through
W. 11th St. Park. I bring my notebook and do some
scribbling. A poem is festering in my imagination.

End of week of 5/2

After a good, long weekend with my Lady,
Monday I set off for Sugar Land as I have a
dermatologist appointment. The guy burns off
five precancerous lesions. (Yes, I'm falling to pieces).

Get to the Cap around 3 PM. Even coming in that
tardy, it's a long day. Bills about water, emergency
protocol during a declared disaster. An arsenal of
amendments circle like birds of prey. But the
humdinger is the bill to kill Critical Race Theory.
The author hasn't the intellect to deflect the mob
of Democrats that circle like buzzards. But I do
applaud him for his courage. As should be expected,
supporters leave him to languish like Prometheus.
Still, the bill passes. We gavel out just before 2 AM.

Tuesday starts early. I'm very tired, but that's the
way it goes. More of the same. Points of Order,
amendments and endless proselytizing. Mercy comes
early, as we leave by 7 PM.

Wednesday we sit and watch as the floor sits
static with Points of Order eternal. I spend much
of my time in the Senate. Getting what's left of
our agenda as close to the finish line as possible.
Leave at 10 PM.

Thursday is the beast. The House has until midnight to
hear all Second Readings on the Calendar. Most bills
will die, and with it the immense amount of work

it takes to get a bill that far. But the unadulterated truth is that most bills need to die. We pass too many laws. It is absurd. The tribe is led by immature frat boys and their hand-picked operatives. They have culled their agenda and it's now a chunk of stinky cheese that will have little to no effect on reality—done to buffer reelection. The tragedy of it all is that the small tweaks and innovative ideas languish in the churning bucket. The tragedy is that the wrong bills are left to rot. Laugh or cry it makes no difference. I just want to get out of here and see the sunlight before I die too.

But Friday breaks in our favor. The bill load is merciful and we get to get out of Dodge by mid-afternoon. Stay in ATX.
Hangout with friends. Hit Half Price Books on N. Lamar. Snag a first edition hardback of Walker Percy's *Lancelot*. Sleep late.

End of week of 5/9

With only two weeks left all eyes turn to the light
and warmth at the end of the proverbial tunnel. We have a
few bills over in the Senate that seem to be moving well.
With the remaining House bills now dead, we hear only
Senate bills. Emergencies flare up from time to time.
A Zoom call with the Comptroller is a bit disenchanting.
Seems we'll never get our Pensions study.

Monday night and into Tuesday I grapple with
getting a bill through the Senate that has massive
consequences should it fail. In fact a multimillion
dollar hotel convention center may be hanging in the balance.
I've been working with a lobbyist since the beginning
of session and we are both ready for the ink to dry.

Thursday is bizarre. We are expecting to work through the
weekend. I make a trip down S. Congress to the chiropractor.

When I come back the House has adjourned until Sunday at
1 PM.
An unexpected weekend! But wait! This is a battle to the
death.
The House and Senate are playing a game over who will kill
whose bills. Who will blink first? We could lose all our hard
work.
Not sure what to do.

Not knowing I make an impromptu visit to see Sandra.
It is a magical two days of reprieve. Saturday we pop in
to Torchy's for drinks and queso. After lunch we walk
through the intermittent rain to an antique store on 19th St.
in the heart of the Height's Historic District.
There I find a super rare, Super Deluxe Box set of Led
Zeppelin's, *CODA*.

End of week 5/16

MARATHON TO THE END

I've only paid attention to the legislature like one
would pay attention to a pesky nat. As far as I can
tell the chamber wars have cooled and we're back in
business. Our strike is over?

Sunday I'm off for a long, long week. The flag
of Sine Die can be seen snapping over the parapets.
But first we must besiege them. The walls are high.

Our hotel bill has passed out of the Senate Natural
Resources and Eco. Dev. Committee unanimously.
It lives!

Our floodplain bill that was killed by a grease ball
lobbyist, was resuscitated in the Senate as an amendment.
It lives! Still a bit of a way to go but it will hinder a form
of predatory lending that targets non-English speaking
peoples.
Late night.

Monday is more wrangling over red meat. Only a week to
go...

And Monday night things start to go down. Hard.
The floor is the floor at this point: long hours in limbo
as we wait for the parliamentarian to determine...
you guessed it...Points of Order! These long hours are
interrupted by fits of bill passages. But they never last.
So, the boys decide to order food as we're headed straight
into the darkness of another long night. They order Cane's,

a rot gut fried chicken place. Little do I know how rot gut it
is. I drink a bit, and chat with a staffer from another office
I've been chatting with a lot lately. His name is Taylor,
and he is another bright young man, too bright in the mind
to be born into the threshold of darkness. We talk of
anthropology,
the history of the Middle East, poetry and philosophy, etc.
At some point, after eating my chicken, I start to feel bad.
I leave the Capitol around midnight. When I get to my apt.
I get very ill. Vomiting ensues till 4 AM.

In the morning I wake and feel as if I have an anvil tied
to my ankle. I feel like I have a fever. I can't hardly get
out of bed. I call in sick—first time in years. The guys
are kind enough to bring me some provisions: soup, water
and a thermometer. I have a 102 fever. I'm down.

I still feel like shit Tuesday morning, but I have to go to
work. Much has misfired in my absence. To begin with
the Rep. is pissed and taking part in a legislative terrorist
movement to kill the bills of Dems who killed a Republican
bill the night before. The dead bill deals with transgenders
in female sports. In reaction, the Dems start to kill
Republican
Senate bills. It's a melee. In retaliation, the Senate start
killing
House bills with impunity. Everything we had going is gone.

The rest of the week is a standoff. Ills of all kinds claim the
respective chambers. All my work is putrefying in the crypt.

It's hard to care about any of it at this point. I just want to go home.

We work through the weekend and make it to Sine Die, which is Memorial Day. Fitting I think. I feel like it's slowing, the blood that beats inside of me…though it pounds like the sea against the cleft cliffs I've never seen, and probably never will.

So why do I return to this den of iniquity again and again? You (Texas) are as a great unrequited love whose repudiation feeds my inspiration. You have become my imagination's blood.
I wasted it all on you, Texas. So build your nest with my spilling guts. It is from your larder that I have bought the food
that fills their coils. Build your nest, weave it well…with the fibers
of my tissue, rancorous and foul…as your table.

AT THE CONCLUSION OF THE 87ᵀᴴ LEGISLATURE

I return to you work weary and with much remorse.
The multitudinous scars, which are indiscernible,
Pock me like a ghost smudges a familiar space
Adorned with wonders from a kinder age.

A familiar space is defined as the times I've spent at
The altar of your bed, pool side, table,
and amid the buds of your born-again
garden. And the kinder…? the ductile touch
Of your sight, light, taste, and organic form.

Sleep is required for this phantom scar to find its peace,
because a place of peace is as remote as the place I
have returned from. Presence and absence
are not opposites…but need morning to merge.

MHM

5/31/21 (Sine Die)

MATT MINOR presently serves as a Chief of Staff in the Texas House of Representatives. In the Texas House he has served under the Pensions Committee, Government Efficiency and Reform, Investments and Financial Services, Bond Indebtedness, Ways and Means, County Affairs and Corrections. He has worked as a political campaign manager and is a public speaker. Matt has authored official state publications, oversees syndicated editorials, (both political and cultural) and is a speech writer and district radio legislative commentator. Prior to his life in state politics, Matt was a professional musician and entertainer. Matt's hobbies are centered on the arts, including the craft of poetry, an interest that has brought academic recognition and numerous awards.

His first novel, *The Representative* was an Amazon Political Fiction Bestseller the summer of 2015 and was accepted and archived into the Texas State Legislative Library. In April of 2016 *The Representative* won an IPPY Gold Medal for South Region Fiction. He has published three subsequent novels, *The District Manager, The Water Lord,* and *The Singular Passion.*

Matt Minor lives a vagabond's life. Sometimes he resides on his ranch property in Wharton County, Texas, sometimes at his apartment in district, or in Austin during legislative session. But he always finds his way back to the home in Houston of the woman he loves, Sandra.

www.ingramcontent.com/pod-product-compliance
Lightning Source LLC
LaVergne TN
LVHW091219080426
835509LV00009B/1072